T0103860

Straight
From
Grandma's
Kitchen

Straight From *Grandma's* Kitchen

MARYANN SADLER

Order this book online at www.trafford.com
or email orders@trafford.com

Most Trafford titles are also available at major online book retailers.

Printed in the United States of America.

ISBN: 978-1-4907-1181-2 (sc)
ISBN: 978-1-4907-1180-5 (e)

Trafford rev. 08/13/2013

 www.trafford.com

North America & international
toll-free: 1 888 232 4444 (USA & Canada)
fax: 812 355 4082

DEDICATED TO MY CHILDREN, MARIANN, KENNY, ROBERT AND SHARITY.

STRAIGHT FROM GRANDMA MARY'S KITCHEN WITH LOVE

AS YOU ARE MEASURING, SUBSTITUTING ONE INGREDIENT FOR ANOTHER ONE, REMEMBER TO PICK UP A WEEKLY PAPER AND STRETCH YOUR DOLLARS BY CLIPPING COUPONS.

Coupons are money. Clip everything, whether you need it this week or next. Most have a month's life to them. Watch the sale bills for what is on sale, match your coupons to the sale items. If you just go buy because you have a coupon for that item, you want benefit by it, unless it is something you need at the moment. Buy only what is on sale and only if you have a coupon. Most items, you can get almost free if you follow that rule.

If you get something free by using your coupon, go for it. If you don't need the item, someone else might. Sock up with your sale items and use the products for baskets to welcome a new neighbor, new baby, a birthday gift, wedding shower, or make that extra Christmas basket, etc.

Couponing is time consuming and work, but it is fun to watch the savings pile up. Once a month, go through your coupons and pick out the expired ones. Yes, you will have expired ones, but think of that item on sale you could have gotten free, if only you had cut out that coupon you saw in last week's paper. Yes, cut out everything.

Instead of buying expensive detergent to wash delicate fabrics, use a small amount of your favorite shampoo that contains conditioner. It works marvelously.

If on a day you feel crappy, you can either wait until something makes you feel better, or figure out what is making you that way and turn the day around. It will be more pleasant for you and everyone else you come in contact with.

In the summer you can grow all these vegetables that you wish to, but in the winter you can make sure you grow more vegetables when it becomes time to plant. What I do all winter is, when I peel potatoes or any other vegetable, I scatter the peelings on the spot where I make my garden. I do this from November through February. I also throw egg shells and coffee grounds (anything that doesn't have salt) where I plan on making the garden. I quit after February as that is close to time for bugs to start and we don't need that. In the spring, when you plow your garden, all those things you fed it with will be plowed in and that makes great fertilizer.

VALUABLE HINTS

1. ½ cup cocoa = 2 squares of unsweetened chocolate
2. When using self-rising baking powder in a recipe, calling for all-purpose flour, omit baking powder it calls for in the recipe. Omit salt also.
3. Scalloped vegetables= vegetables cooked in white sauce.
4. 1 oz. (1 square) of chocolate = 3 tablespoons cocoa.
5. If pie crust edges brown too quickly. Cover with strips of foil.

BREADS

CAKES

CANDY

CANNING

CASSEROLLS

COOKIES

DESSERTS

DIPS

DRESSINGS

DRINKS

MEAT

PIES

SALADS

SNACKS

SOUPS

VEGETABLES

DRESSINGS

HOMEMADE SALAD DRESSING

⅓ cup cider vinegar

⅓ cup sugar

13 cup oil

Mix sugar and vinegar until sugar dissolves.

Stir in oil

Refrigerate, and shake before using.

FRENCH DRESSING

½ cup ketchup

½ cup corn oil

¼ cup apple cider vinegar

2 or 3 teaspoons powdered sugar

1 clove garlic split

¼ teaspoon salt

Dash of black pepper

Combine ingredients in a jar. Cover and shake very well. Chill. Remove garlic. Shake again before using.

FRENCH DRESSING

1 cup sugar	2 teaspoons paprika
¾ cup ketchup	1 teaspoon diced garlic
½ cup cider vinegar	1 graded very fine onion
1 cup vegetable oil	2 teaspoon salt

Mix in blender and keep in refrigerator

BREAKFAST

HOMEMADE PANCAKE SYRUP

Heat 1 cup of water to boil. Turn the heat down and stir in 1 lb. of brown sugar. Continue to stir until the sugar has completely melted. Great served hot over sausage and pan cakes.

DRINKS

ORANGE LEMONADE

2 quarts water
1 can (12 oz.) frozen orange juice, thawed
1 can (12 oz.) frozen lemonade, thawed
1 cup sugar

In a saucepan heat water and sugar until sugar is dissolved, stirring constantly.
Cool
Transfer to a large pitcher, stir in the thawed juices.
Chill.

PUNCH

Bottle of ginger ale
Can of pineapple juice
Can of orange juice
Stir in a half gallon of sherbet ice cream
Slice an orange and let orange slices float on top

STRAWBERRY SHAKE
Any berry can be used

Blend a pint of berries in a 2 quart blender until nearly smooth.

Add one half cup sugar. Blend again, until sugar is really mixed in.

Using a spoon to dip ice cream, so it won't be in a large piece,

Add the ½ gal carton Vanilla ice cream.

Blend until mixed.

Pour into a glass, grab a straw and enjoy.

VEGETABLES

SPICED ACORN SQUASH

6 acorn squash cut in half
¾ cup brown sugar 2 teaspoons cinnamon
1 teaspoon nutmeg
½ teaspoon cloves
1-½ cups melted butter

Preheat oven to 400 degrees. Remove seeds from squash. Place each squash in a pan, peeling side down. Combine all the above ingredients and mix well. Pour the mixture in each squash. Cover with foil and bake from 1 to ½ hours.

STUFFED JALAPENO PEPPERS

1 pk. Cream cheese
(8 oz. softened)

3 tablespoons bacon bits

1 cup shredded sharp
cheddar cheese

12 jalapeno peppers

⅓ cup flour   2 eggs slightly beaten

½ cup bread crumbs   vegetable oil to fry

Mix cream cheese, cheddar cheese and bacon bits.
Firmly press a heaping teaspoon full of cheese mix in each pepper half.
Cover and chill for one hour.
Place flour, eggs and bread crumbs in three separate bowls.
Dip peppers in flour, then the eggs and then the bread crumbs coating good with each.
Fry a few at a time.
Drain on paper towels.

POTATOES FOR THE GRILL

Coat the aluminum foil with cooking spray
Arrange some bacon in the center of the foil. Top with a few thin sliced potatoes, some chopped green bell peppers, some chopped onions and some cheddar cheese. Top with a few more potatoes, peppers and onions. Sprinkle with salt and black pepper,. Add a little more cheese and bacon.
Top all of this with another layer of aluminum foil sprayed with nonstick cooking spray. Seal both pieces of aluminum foil together, with a small slit in the top foil to let some steam escape. Usually takes about 25 minutes for it to cook.

BEST MASHED POTATOES

Mash potatoes as usual.
While still hot, stir in desired amount of butter.
Layer with cheese,
Layer with chopped green onions,
Sprinkle with small amt. of salt and garlic salt,
Layer this with bacon bits.
Sit out sour cream for those that like sour cream

COLE SLAW

Shred the cabbage or purchase a small bag shredded.
Add ¼ cup oil
½ cup sugar
Two tablespoons vinegar
And stir in enough mayo to make it creamy.
Let sit in frig. For 1 hour.
Sugar amt. can be reduced.

BAKED BEANS

Two cans of pork and beans any brand.
Small onion diced
Tablespoon mustard
½ cup barbecue sauce or ketchup
4 slices of bacon cut into small pieces.

Brown bacon in skillet, stir in the onion and stir until onion is tender and bacon not burned.

Add beans, and the remaining ingredients.

You can either bake them in the oven 350 for 20 minutes, or on top of stove. If on top of stove, stir occasionally and cook until most of moisture is gone. About 10 minutes.

GREEN BEANS

Two cans of green beans or fresh. Fresh will take a little longer to cook

Put beans in a pot. I love my iron pot for this.

Dice a small onion, add to the beans.

Cut a couple strips of bacon in small pieces, add to the pot.

Salt to taste

Cook about 20 min.

TURNIPS

You can either slice or quarter them. They cook a lot like stewed potatoes.

Add a small amt. of sugar, a dash of salt and pepper.

Boil on low heat until tender.

FRIED TURNIPS

Shred turnips like hash browns.
Add shortening to skillet.
Let shortening warm a little.
Add turnips.
Add small amt. of sugar.
Add a dash of salt and black pepper.

MASHED TURNIPS

Peel and quarter. Cook as cooking potatoes.
Add salt, pepper and butter.
Mash as mashing potatoes

TURNIP SLAW

Make as making cabbage slaw
Yes I and my family likes turnips.

STUFFED JALAPENO PEPPERS

BE SURE TO WEAR GLOVES PREPARING THESE

Cut the end from about 15 jalapeno peppers.
Slice the peppers in half, length wise.
Scrape all the seeds out.

Rinse the peppers in cool water.

Brown ½ pound sausage and drain and crumble the sausage.

Mix sausage, a pkg. of Mexican type cheese, a 1 pkg. cream cheese,

Stuff the peppers with the sausage mixture and cheese mixture.

Bake 350 degrees about 25 minutes.

SIDE DISHES

Mash cooked carrots into potatoes as you mash the potatoes.

Add sautéed onions to mashed potatoes

Pan Fry your greens in bacon grease

Stir cheese into cooked rice while the rice is still hot.

Slice an onion in rings, roll in flour and deep fry until golden brown

Roll sliced dill pickles in flour and deep fry as you would squash

Boil squash, tomatoes and 1 hot pepper together until the squash is tender.

POTATOE BAKE

2 cups of grated potatoes

1 cup sour cream

1 can cream mushroom soup or cream of chicken soup

MaryAnn Sadler

¼ cup butter softened
2 packages of grated cheese
¼ cup melted butter

Preheat oven to 350
Mix potatoes, sour cream, soup, butter and cheese in a bowl. Spread in a baking dish and pour the ¼ cup melted butter over the mixture. Bake about 1 hour.

ONION ROASTED POTATOES

1 onion soup mix pk.
⅓ cup oil
Potatoes cut in small chunks
Roast at 450 for about 40 minutes

POLK

Bob's favorite

Fresh, boil 10 minutes, pour off water, add fresh water, salt and bacon grease and cook 20 min. Fix a pot of beans and a big pan of cornbread to go with this dish. If polk is frozen, thaw it out, just put in pan with a small amount of water and seasoning, cook and serve.

CASSEREOLES

POTATOE CASSEROLE

2 lb. bag of frozen has browns
2 - 16 oz. boxes sour cream
2 cans mushroom soup
1 stick butter
Small onion
8 oz. shredded cheese, (I like cheddar.)
Mix all ingredients together, pour in a baking dish and bake at 350 until light brown.
You can put French fried onions or cornflakes on top after it is baked. I prefer the onions as cornflakes will get soggy.

CAULIFLOWER SUPREME
(One of Mariann's favorites)

1 med. Cauliflower broke up into small pieces
1 can cream mushroom soup

½ cup shredded cheese
Cook cauliflower 10 minutes in small amt. of water
In a casserole dish, alternate layers of cauliflower, soup and cheese. Repeat until all is used up. Bake 350 for 15 minutes

BROCOLI CASSEROLE

½ stick margarine

1 onion chopped fine

1 small jar cheese whiz

2 bunches broccoli, chopped fine.

1 can cream mushroom soup 1 cup minute rice

Melt margarine in skillet.
Add onions and cook until onion turns clear
Stir in broccoli and mushroom soup
Simmer for 5 min.
Mix in Cheese whiz and rice. Bake in oven 300 for 20 minutes.

CORNBREAD CASSEROLE
(Deven's Favorite)

Preheat oven to 375

½ cup melted butter
1 - 16 oz. box sour cream

1 egg
1 can whole kernel corn (drained)
1 can cream style corn (do not drain)
Continued next page
1 can cream corn
1 pkg. Jiffy corn muffin mix
2 cup shredded cheese, (I like cheddar)

Mix altogether, except for 1 cup of cheese. Bake about 45 minutes. Pour the remaining 1 cup of cheese over top. Cook additional 10 to 15 minutes until the cheese on top begins to melt.

CORN CAKES

1 can of creamed corn
1 box of jiffy muffin mix
1 egg
Mix together, drop by teaspoons full into oil and deep fry to a golden brown

AS YOU SEE, I LIKE CHEESE.
HERE IS ONE OF MY FAVORITES

CHEESE BALLS

2 (8 oz. pkgs.) Cream cheese
2 small pkgs. beef chopped very fine

5 green onions, (green tops only) chopped very fine
1 tablespoons Worcestershire sauce

Mix altogether and shape into a ball
Roll in crushed nuts.
Serve with Ritz crackers

The white part of the onion that is left can be diced and frozen for later use in another dish of sort.

If you find two of the same recipe in this book, it is just a freebie for you.

MEATS

CHICKEN POT PIE
Sharity's Favorite

Boil chicken until it falls from bone easily.
Remove chicken from broth and place into a separate pan or bowl to cool.
In broth, place a 16 oz. bag of frozen vegetables and heat to boil.
Lower the heat to simmer.

In a small bowl, mix well ¼ cup flour, one teaspoon each of salt and black pepper
Add enough cool water to make a thin paste.

Stir the mixture of flour, salt and pepper, slowly into the simmering broth and vegetables.
Stir until it starts to thicken. Remove from heat, tear chicken from bone and add the chicken to the vegetable mixture. Taste to see if salty enough for your taste.

Line a pan or baking dish with a small amt. of pie crust. Based on how much crust you want on the bottom of your pie. Pour the vegetable mixture into the lined pan or baking dish. Top with pie crust. Sprinkle a little pepper on top, bake at 350 approx. 45 minutes. Keep check on it, as you don't want your crust to burn. Remember, the mixture has already been cooked. Just bake until crust is light golden brown.

CHICKEN AND DUMPLINGS
(The whole family's favorite)

Boil chicken until it can easily be torn off the bone.
When chicken is done, remove it from the broth and put it in a pan or bowl to cool. Salt the broth to suit your taste, keep it simmering. Add a small amt. of yellow food coloring to the broth. Based on how yellow you want your dumplings. Take a bowl and put flour in it, making a well in the middle of the flour, place an egg or two in the well, depends on how many dumplings you want to make. Add a pinch of baking powder, 1 cup of water. Mix with your hands until it is a dry enough ball to handle.
Place aluminum foil or something on the table, or counter, to roll the dough out on.
Pinch a hand full of dough off and roll it out very thin. I use a pizza cutter, and cut the dough into thin strips. Slowly drop them into the simmering pot of broth
Continue until you have used all your dough up.

Turn burner on low and time 15 minutes.

Tear chicken from the bone, and stir it carefully into the dumplings after the 15 minutes. Stir just enough to mix the chicken in. as you don't want to make mush out of your dumplings. Instead of stirring the chicken into the dumplings, you can just put it a separate bowl and let your guest add as much chicken to the dumplings as they wish.

FRIED DEER MEAT
(Bob's Favorite)

Soak the deer all day in soy sauce.

Cut it up into small thin slices. Add salt and pepper. Roll it in flour, pound the flour into it, roll it again in flour and fry until brown on one side, turn and fry until brown on other side. Drain on paper towels.

BLACK BEANS, RICE AND PORK STEAK
(I love this)

Cut a pound of pork steak into small pieces
Dice a small onion
Dice a hot pepper
Place all of this with a package of black beans in a crock pot, with enough water to cover the beans. Be

sure to wash your beans first. Cook it slow all day, or until the beans are done. It can also be cooked in a pan on top of the stove. Have to watch it if you do, so it want burn. The last 5 minutes of cooking, or 5 minutes before you serve it, stir in a cup of minute rice, or a cup of cooked rice.

CAJUN SAUSAGE AND RICE

1 box (8 oz.) red beans and rice cooked as box direction Sauté 2 bell peppers 5 minutes in 1 teaspoon vegetable oil. Add to the peppers 1 lb. pk. Cajun sausages, cut up into small pieces. Continue sautéing about 3 minutes. Mix the bean rice mixture to the sausage and pepper mixture. Mix all of this with 2 cups of cooked rice.

ENCHILADAS
(One of Sharity's favorites)

1 pound. Ground beef, browned and drained
2 cups shredded cheese, your choice
1 (16 oz.) jar Enchilada Sauce 10 flour (6in) tortillas
To the beef, add ½ cup of the sauce and 1 cup of the cheese.

Put on the center of each tortilla, about 2 tablespoons of the meat mixture. Roll it up and place it with the fold side down in a well-greased pan or baking dish.

Top them with the remaining sauce and cheese. Place into a 350 degree preheated oven and bake about 20 minutes or until the cheese melts.

FRIED CHICKEN

Salt and pepper the chicken. I, also, like to use a small amount of garlic powder or garlic salt. Roll the chicken pieces in flour, coating it well. In a covered skillet, with oil or shortening, your choice, enough to cover half way over the chicken, slowly brown the chicken on one side, turn and brown on the other side. Using a fork to hold on to the chicken, choose the thickest piece and with a knife, make a slit in the thickest part. If no pink shows when you press on the piece, the chicken is done. Drain on paper towels.

FRIED SQUIRREL

Make sure to cut the kernels out from under the front legs. Cut up the squirrel,(to tenderize it sprinkle it with lemon juice and let set a couple hours If the squirrel is frozen, you can soak it in the lemon juice while it thaws out.) Then sprinkle with salt and pepper, roll in self-rising flour. If you think the squirrel is an old one, you can sprinkle it good with meat tenderizer, before you roll it in the flour. Fry slowly until brown on one side, turn and brown on other side.

I wrote a poem here, I hope you all enjoy.

SQUIRREL HUNTER

The hunter ties up the old hound.
Says, "Sorry, Blue, but when I go hunting, you have to be bound."
He ties him to the tree.
And says, "When I get back, I'll sit you free".
The hunter hears the deer clanging their antlers together as they fight for what?
Maybe over a mate, their territory, or like two boys saying, "I want what you've got."
He hears the squirrels chatter in the trees,
As if to say, "Hey, we are so free."
But, suddenly a shot rings out,
As the hunter is just about,
To get the limit of the squirrels.
The quail flutters in frenzy
To hid her chicks.
As she calls out to them, "Quick, quick."
As the hunter walks by,
A large snake slitters away.
The lizard looks at the snake and asks, "Can I share your cave?"
The frog laughs as the snake slides into its hole,
And says to the hunter, "Thanks, Man. That snake had me lined up, to be his supper bowl.

The dog chained up, while his master hunts, says to himself, "No doubt,
My Master will come home with squirrels in his pouch.
When he gets here, he will turn me loose.
I will then have fun chasing that old squawking goose".

TORTILLA WRAPS

1 can of chili with beans
½ cup minute rice
Mix together and cook 1 minute (Until rice is done)
Spoon a small amount of this on a small tortilla.
Top with cheese, chopped green onions and chopped tomatoes.
Wrap the tortilla, secure with a toothpick.

Keep warm or warm as you eat them.

CHOP SUEY

½ cup butter
1medium onion chopped fine
1 teaspoon salt
1½ cup celery chopped fine
¼ cup green pepper chopped fine
1 ½ cup hot water

1 medium can Chinese vegetables, drained
2 cups of meat, your choice, cut up into strips and cooked until no pink remains. You can boil it if you like, but I like it sautéed.
2 tablespoons cold water
2 tablespoons cornstarch or 4 tablespoons flour
1 ½ tablespoons soy sauce
1 teaspoon sugar

Melt butter in a large skillet
Add the onion and fry until the onion turns clear
Add salt, celery, green pepper, hot water and if you wish, a dash of black pepper
Cover and cook about 5 minutes.
Add the Chinese vegetables and the meat
Mix this up and cook about 5 minutes.
In a separate bowl, mix the flour or cornstarch with sugar, add soy sauce and cold water and stir this into the cooked mixture. Continue to cook about 1 minute, stirring constantly.

It can be served with hot rice, but I like noodles

PIZZA SOUP
(One of Kenny's favorites.
He'd prefer the mushrooms were left out.)

1 ½ cups sliced mushrooms
½ cup chopped onion

1 teaspoon vegetable oil
1 ½ cup's water
1 15 oz. can of pizza sauce
1 ½ cups chopped pepperoni
1 cup chopped tomatoes, or 1 small can of tomato sauce
¼ cup chopped green peppers
½ cup cooked Italian sausage
¼ teaspoon Italian seasoning
¼ cup grated parmesan cheese
1 cup shredded mozzarella cheese

Sauté mushrooms and onion in the same skillet you browned the sausage until the onion begins to turn clear. (You might not want to use all the grease the sausage left.)
Pour into your slow crock cooker. Add all the other ingredients except the cheeses. Before serving, stir in the parmesan cheese. Top with the mozzarella cheese.

The slow crock on low while you are away, or you can add all the ingredients into the same skillet you cooked the sausage and cook about 20 minutes and serve.

HAM AND BEANS
(Another family favorite)

Soak the beans all night covered with water.
Wash them and put in a colander and run fresh water over them.

I do this because when you just wash them out of the water you soak them in, there will still be some of the wash water on the beans. YUK

If cooking while at work, put them in a crock pot. If you cook them on top of the stove, cover them with water, place a lid on them, bring to a boil and then turn heat to simmer. But, be sure to watch them or they will boil dry and scorch. No one likes scorched beans.

After putting them in the crock pot or pan on top of stove, add about a fourth cup of canned hot peppers with a tablespoon of the juice the peppers were canned in.

The amount of salt and black pepper you use will be your call.

Add one tablespoon of butter or margarine.

If using a crock pot, usually all day on low or about 4 hours, give or take an hour, beans should be done. On top of stove, takes a little longer.

Now make a pan of cornbread and a pan of poke and you have a great country supper.

CASHEW CHICKEN

2 tablespoons cornstarch or 4 tablespoons flour
1 tablespoon brown sugar
1 and ¼ cups chicken broth
2 tablespoons soy sauce
1 and ½ pounds boneless skinless chicken breast, cut up in small pieces.

½ pound sliced mushrooms, or a can of sliced mushrooms. *optional*
1 small green hot pepper
4 green onions cut in small pieces
1 and ½ teaspoon ginger
1 small can sliced water chestnuts
1 cup salted cashews
Hot cooked rice.

Combine cornstarch or flour, with brown sugar, chicken broth and soy sauce. Set this to the side.

In a large skillet stir fry chicken in 2 tablespoon of oil until it is no longer pink in side. Remove from the skillet, but keep it warm. In the same skillet stir fry the mushrooms, green pepper, onions and ginger in 1 tablespoon of oil until the green pepper is just a little crisp. This takes about 5 minutes. Now stir in the chicken, chestnuts and cashews.

Stir the broth mixture and add it to the pan. Bring everything to a boil and cook and stir about 2 minutes. It will begin to get thick. Serve it over your hot rice.

BEEF AND BROCCOLI

Slice about a lb. of boneless beef into thin strips
In a skillet over medium heat, heat 1 tablespoon oil. Add the beef and stir until it is lightly brown and most of the juice has disappeared.
Add 1 can of condensed tomato soup,

3 tablespoons soy sauce
Continued on net page
1 tablespoon apple cider vinegar
1 teaspoon garlic powder
¼ teaspoon crushed red pepper.
Heat to boil.
Add about 3 cups of fresh broccoli or thawed if you use frozen. Cook over medium heat until broccoli is still a little crisp. Stir it often. Serve it over rice.

PEPPER JACK MEATLOAF

Combine together

1 egg
¼ cup chopped onions
Salt
Black pepper
1 and ½ lb. ground beef

Put half the mixture in a loaf pan. Make a dent in the center of the half. Fill the dent full with the shredded pepper jack cheese; Place the other half of the meat mixture on top of the cheese.
Press the sides together to seal in the cheese. Bake at 350 for about 50 minutes. Sprinkle cheese over the meatloaf while it is still hot and let the cheese melt over it.

SAUSAGE BALLS

1 lb. hot sausage
1 lb. cheddar cheese
3 cups Bisquick
Mix together and shape into tiny balls
Bake at 350 for about 30 minutes

GREAT WAY TO FIX LITTLE
SMOKEY SAUSAGES

Wrap each little sausage with a piece of bacon.
Cover with a thin layer of brown sugar.
Bake at 350 degrees until the bacon is crisp, about 20 minutes.
Dip them in your favorite dressing, hot sauce, etc. enjoy.

CAN-CAN CHICKEN
(One of Mariann's favorites)

1 can evaporated milk
1 can condense cream of celery soup
1 cup celery chopped fine.
1 can condense cream chicken soup
1 can condense chicken noodle soup
¼ cup flour
1 can chunk white chicken, drained

1 can Chow Mein noodles

In a large skillet, mix the first five ingredients together. Bring to a boil. Cook and stir until it starts to thicken. Add the chicken, heat until it is hot. Serve over the noodles or put noodles on top; your choice.

OVEN POT ROAST

Sprinkle meat with flour. Pound the flour into the meat slightly.
Mix 1 cup water, a package of onion soup mix, a little Worcestershire sauce and pour over the meat.
Cover and bake at 325 for approx . . . 1 to 1 ½ hours.
Turn the meat, add potatoes, carrots, onions, vegetables your choice, cover and cook approx . . . 45 min. more.

SALISBURY STEAK

Combine 1 egg
½ cup dry bread crumbs
½ cup tomato juice.
1 tablespoon minced onion
1 lb. ground beef
Shape into patties, brow in skillet.
Add an envelope of gravy mix, I cup water. Simmer covered 10 minutes.

POTATOES WITH FRANKS

8 hot dogs   2 cups seasoned mashed potatoes
½ cup grated cheese   Dash of paprika

Slit hot dogs lengthwise almost all the way through.
Spread open,.
Place cut side up on greased baking sheet.
Heap mashed potatoes on the hot dogs, filling them as
much as possible.
Sprinkle with grated cheese and paprika and heat for
15 minutes at 400 degrees.

QUICK SHEPARD PIE

1 lb. ground beef
1 can stewed tomatoes
Instant mashed potatoes
1 can mixed vegetables
Salt and pepper to taste, any spices you wish.

Preheat oven 400.
Brown beef and drain
Add tomatoes, salt. Pepper and other spices you desire.
Prepare the mashed potatoes while the meat is cooking.
Add the vegetables to the meat.
Put in casserole dish.
Top with potatoes.
Bake 12 minutes or until potatoes are lightly brown.

BREADS

FAST DINNER ROLLS

1 cup warm water
1 pkg. Yeast
4 tablespoons shortening
¼ cup sugar
1 teaspoon salt
2 cups flour

Dissolve the yeast in the warm water.
Mix all the other ingredients together.
Add to the yeast, stir until smooth.
Set aside and let double in size.
Knead down
Place on floured surface, pat down until thickness of biscuits.
Cut out the rolls and place in a well-greased muffin pan, let rise.
Bake at 350 degrees for about 20 or 30 minutes. Keep watch on them so they want burn.

BANANA NUT BREAD
(Jennifer can eat this anytime)

1 stick of butter or margarine, room temp
1 cup of sugar
Pinch of salt
1 teaspoon baking powder
2 beaten eggs
3 very ripe bananas, smashed
2 cups flour
½ cup chopped walnuts

Mix baking powder, flour, sugar and salt together.
Stir in the eggs, bananas, butter and walnuts
Pour into a greased baking bread pan.
Bake at 350 for 1 hour and approximately10 minutes
Based on what size pans you use. Test with toothpicks
doesn't always work.
The touch on top if it doesn't leave a finger print is
good.

BANANA BREAD (NO NUTS)

3 eggs
2 cups sugar
¾ cup shortening
3 cups all-purpose flour

1 ½ teaspoon baking soda
½ teaspoon salt
1 teaspoon vanilla
2 cups mashed ripe bananas

Mix all dry ingredients together
Stir in eggs and bananas
Beat well by hand.
Pour into greased bread pan. Bake one hour at 325
If tooth pick does not come out clean at end of baking time, turn temp to 350. Bake 10 minutes and check with tooth pick again. Repeat 10 minutes a time if needed to get done.

MONKEY BREAD
(This is very delicious)

3 cans biscuits
1 tablespoon cinnamon mixed with ½ cup sugar
1 stick butter or margarine
1 cup brown sugar
2 teaspoons water
½ cup chopped nuts

Cut the biscuits into 4 pieces
Roll each piece in the cinnamon sugar mixture
Put the nuts in the bottom of a greased bunt pan.
Place the coated biscuits on top of the nuts.
Melt the butter or marg.
Add the brown sugar and water.
Boil for 2 minutes stirring.
Pour the boiled mixture over the top of the biscuits.
Bake at 350 for about 25 minutes.

HOLIDAY PUMPKIN BREAD

2 eggs
1 ¼ cups sugar
⅛ teaspoon nutmeg
¼ teaspoon salt
1 cup cooked pumpkin or 1 small can
½ cup vegetable oil
1 ½ cups flour
1 teaspoon baking soda
½ teaspoon cinnamon
1 ½ cups chopped nuts
½ cup candied cherries chopped fine

Combine eggs, oil and pumpkin with ⅓ cup water.
Mix all the dry ingredients together
Beat this into the pumpkin mixture
Stir in the nuts and cherries. Pour into a greased and floured pan.
Bake at 350 for about one hour.

ZUCCHINI BREAD

3 ½ cups all-purpose flour 1 cup oil
1 teaspoon salt 3 beaten eggs
3 teaspoons cinnamon 3 teaspoons vanilla
1 teaspoon baking soda 2 ½ cups grated zucchini
¼ teaspoon baking powder
2 ½ cups sugar

Stir together all the dry ingredients.

Add remaining ingredients.

Add 1 cup nuts.

Bake in greased pan approx. 1 hour at 350.

If tooth pick doesn't come out clean reduce temp to 300 and check bread every 10 min. until tooth pick comes out clean.

CHERRY NUT BREAD

2 ½ cups flour, all-purpose

2 Tablespoons grated orange peel

1 ¼ cups sugar

¼ can tart cherries, drained

1 Tablespoon baking powder

and coarsely chopped

7 Tablespoon veg. shortening

½ cup chopped nuts

3 eggs

1 cup orange juice

Preheat oven to 350

Grease 2 loaf pans.

Combine flour, sugar, baking powder.

Mix in shortening.

Stir in eggs, orange juice, orange peel and cherry juice.

Fold in cherries and nuts.

Bake 45 minutes or until toothpick comes out clean.

QUICK SUPPER BREAD

3 cups flour
1 heaping tablespoon baking powder
1 ½ teaspoon salt
1 ½ cup milk
½ cup margarine

Combine dry ingredients.
Combine milk and ⅓ cup margarine.
Add to the flour mixture, mixing just until moistened.
Spread into a greased 13 by 9 inch pan. Brush with the remaining margarine.
Bake at 400 degrees for 25 to 30 min. or, until golden brown.
Cut and serve warm.

PUMPKIN BREAD

Mix together
1 cup oil
3 cups sugar
3 eggs
1 can or 2 cups pumpkin

In separate bowl
Mix together
3 cups flour
1 teaspoon cloves

1 teaspoon cinnamon
1 teaspoon nutmeg
1 teaspoon baking soda
½ teaspoon salt
1 teaspoon baking powder
Add to pumpkin mixture
Stir in ½ cup nuts
Bake in 2 greased loaf pans 1 hour 350 or toothpick test.
Very good if garnished with glazed. (Powdered sugar and, milk)
Also makes a pretty Bundt bread

LEMON POPPYSEED BREAD

1 pkg. lemon cake mix 4 eggs
1 pkg. instant lemon pudding, (1 pie size) ½ cup oil
1 cup water ⅛ cup poppy seeds
Bake at 350 until golden brown.

SOUPS

BROCCOLI SOUP

4 small stalks celery chopped
1 onion chopped
3 tablespoons butter
2 bunches broccoli chopped
3 cups chicken broth
2 teaspoons garlic salt
½ teaspoon black pepper
4 tablespoons flour or 2 tablespoons cornstarch
¼ cup water
Sauté celery and onion in butter until the celery is tender
Add broccoli, broth, garlic salt and black pepper
Simmer about 45 minutes.
Mix flour or cornstarch with water, cook and stir until it starts to get thick. Add this to the broccoli mixture

CREAM OF BROCCOLI SOUP

1 small pkg. of frozen chopped broccoli
1 can of mushroom soup
1 ½ cup cream or milk
2 tablespoons butter.
Salt and pepper to taste
Cook Broccoli in a small amt. of water until tender, drain. (Here I like to save the liquid and put it in a boil to add vegetables to later and when the bowl gets full of small amts. of left over vegetables each day, I have the making of an excellent other kind of soup.)

Mix the mushroom soup with the milk or cream, stir constantly while heating.
Don't boil. Milk will burn.
Add the broccoli, pepper, and butter. Heat just to bubble

POTATOE SOUP
(Grandpa Burton's Favorite)

2 stalks celery chopped
1 small onion chopped
5 to 6 med. Potatoes, peeled or not, diced
1 can chicken broth
1 soup can water
1 can cream or for a lighter soup use milk

8 oz. sour cream
1 teaspoon parsley flakes
Salt and pepper to taste
Cook on med. Heat until vegetables or tender

FREEZER SOUP

Place a bowl in the freezer and when you have, maybe just a spoon of corn or other vegetables left over from a meal, put it in this bowl and keep adding to it. Even bits of steak or roast, and even the gravy from the roast left over, can be added to it. When the bowl gets full, you have the makings of a very delicious soup. You can always add tomatoes, okra, or whatever you desire to it to make it sooooooo good.

DESERTS

APPLE CRISP
(One of my favorites)

Slice 4 or 5 apples into a 9 inch square baking dish
that has been buttered or sprayed With cooking spray.
Sprinkle with a mixture of ½ cup sugar.

> ½ cup water
>
> 1 teaspoon cinnamon
>
> 1 teaspoon nutmeg

Cut ½ cup butter into ¾ cup oatmeal

> ¾ cup brown sugar
>
> ¼ cup flour
>
> 1 teaspoon cinnamon

Pour this mixture over the apple mixture and bake at
350 for about 1 hour. You can serve with ice cream or
whip cream

PINEAPPLE DESSERT

Empty 1 box of angel food cake mix into a large bowl. Fold in 1 (16 oz.) can of pineapple, with juice, and 1 teaspoon of vanilla.

Pour this into an un-greased 9 by 13 in. pan. Bake at 350 for about 30 minutes or until golden brown.

NUT SURPRISE
(One of Mariann's favorites)

¾ cup sugar
½ cup chopped pecans
1 regular size can sweetened crushed pineapple, drained
1 regular size can sweetened fruit cocktail, drained
1 can cheery pie filling
2 cup size Cool Whip.

In a large bowl, partially mash fruit cocktail and cherry pie filling. Mix in pecans sugar and pineapple. Fold in Cool Whip and refrigerate until ready to serve.

TIP: When draining the fruit, drain it in a cup. Drink the juice. It's good for you. LOL. Love ya.

CRANBERRY RELISH
(GREAT FOR CHRISTMAS)

Grind up 2 red apples
> 2 oranges with white part and seeds removed
> 1 package (16oz.) cranberries
> 1 cup celery

Stir in 1 small can of crushed pineapple, including the juice.

Dissolve I small pkg. of raspberry Jell-O in 1 cup boiling water. Stir 1 cup of sugar into the dissolved Jell-O. Add this to the ground up mixture Stir in 1 cup of chopped walnuts. Refrigerator over night.

HELLO DOLLIES

1 stick of butter melted in a 9x9 pan.

1 cup graham cracker crumbs

1 cup coconut

1 cup chocolate chips

1 cup chopped nuts. (I like walnuts)

1 cup Eagle Brand milk

Sprinkle the graham cracker crumbs over the melted butter.

Layer the other ingredients. Pour the milk over all this. Bake at 350 for 30 minutes.

APPLE FRITTERS
(One of Deven's favorites)

Leave the apple whole, but dig the core out of 2 sour apples, but don't peel.
Slice them in rings.

Mix together ⅔ cups flour
1 tablespoon powdered sugar
¼ teaspoon baking powder
½ teaspoon lemon peel or 1 teaspoon lemon juice. If you use the lemon juice make sure all the powder ingredients are mixed together before you add the juice.

In a separate bowl beat 1 egg
½ cup milk
1 teaspoon oil
Add the egg mixture to the flour mixture, beat until smooth. Dip the apple rings in the batter.
Deep fry until golden brown.
I like to sprinkle the warm fritters with powdered sugar.

CHERRY NUT SALAD
(One Of Mariann's Favorites)

Mix 1 small pkg. of cherry Jell-O with 1 (8oz.) pkg. cream cheese
Add 1 cup hot water. Beat until foamy.

Fold in 1 cup pecans, or walnuts, your choice, and 1
can pineapple, with juice.
Pour into a mold of your choice and refrigerate

STRAWBERRY AND CRÈME DESSERT

Crust
1 pack sugar cookie mix
½ cup butter or marg. Softened
1 egg

Filling
1 cup white baking chips
1 small pkg. cream cheese, softened

Topping
1 cup crushed strawberries
3 cups sliced strawberries
½ cup sugar
2 Tablespoons cornstarch or 4 Tablespoons flour
⅓ cup water

Oven 350 degrees
Lightly grease or spray bottom of a 13x9 glass dish
Mix together cookie mix, butter or margarine, and egg
to a soft ball.
Press this into the baking dish.

Bake about 20 minutes or until it turns a light golden brown.

Cool completely

Place baking chips in microwave about 60 seconds until melted.

In a separate bowl beat the cream cheese on medium speed until smooth. Stir the melted chips into the cream cheese.

Spread this mixture over the crust. Cool in frig.

In a pan, mix sugar, cornstarch or flour, which ever you used.

Add the strawberries that have been crushed and the water.

Cook stirring constantly until it boils and gets thick.

Let this set about 10 minutes to cool.

Stir in the sliced strawberries and pour this over the chip and cheese mixture in the baking dish.

Keep in frig. Until ready to serve

FROZEN WALDORF SALAD
(One Of Son-in-law Jim's Favorite)

1 reg. size can crushed pineapple
1 cup sugar
2 well beaten eggs

Pinch of salt
1 cup celery, chopped fine
2 med. Red apples, chopped fine
1 cup chopped pecans
1 cup cool whip or small carton
Drain the pineapple, save the juice
Mix the juice, sugar, eggs and salt together. Cook stirring constantly until it begins to get thick. Cool this completely. Mix in the cool whip, put in a freezer bowl and freeze until firm.

SNOW CREAM

2 cans light cream, chilled
2 ¼ cups sugar
2 Tablespoons vanilla
Pinch of salt
3 well beaten eggs, optional, but best if you use them.
Mix this altogether, and then stir in the snow.

DIRT

2 cups milk
1 large pkg. chocolate pudding mix
1 (8oz.) container cool whip
1 (16 oz. pack) Oreo cookies

Crush cookies and divide in half.

Make the pudding according to pkg. directions and let cool 5 minutes

Stir the cool whip and half of the cookies into the pudding, mixing until it is about the same color.

Place enough of the remaining cookies in the bottom of a clean, new, never used flower pot. to cover the bottom

Fill the pot with the pudding mixture and top off with the remaining cookies. Chill about 1 hour. Decorate with flowers or gummy worms. Can be served with a small trowels instead of spoons.

PUMPKIN DESERT

1 can of plain pumpkin
1 can evaporated milk
3 eggs
1cup sugar
4 teaspoons pumpkin pie spice
1 box Super Moist vanilla cake mix
1 and ½ cups chopped walnuts
¾ cup margarine melted
Cool Whip

Heat oven to 350

I like to use a glass baking dish. 13 by 9
Grease or spray bottom and sides.
In a bowl, beat the pumpkin, milk, sugar pumpkin pie spice until smooth.
Pour this into the baking dish.
Sprinkle the cake mix over the pumpkin mixture. Sprinkle the walnuts over the cake mix. Pour the melted butter over the walnuts.
Bake approx. 50 minutes are until the tooth pick test.
Best if served warm.

DR.PEPPER SALAD

Pour ½ of a 2 liter of Dr. Pepper in a pan.
Heat just to boiling point.

Dissolve 2 small pkgs. or 1 large pkg. of cherry Jell-O in the Dr. Pepper.
Stir real good to dissolve the Jell-O
Add the other half of the 2 litter.
Add 1 cup of drained crushed pineapple
Add I cup of chopped pecans
Chill until set.

COLA SALAD

1 reg. size can of cherries, drained, saving the juice.
1 reg. size can of crushed pineapple, drained, saving the juice.
Heat the juice just to boil.
Dissolve 1 small pkg. of cherry Jell-O in the juice.
Stir until Jell-O is dissolved.
Add 1 can of coke.
Refrigerate over night
Stir in the nuts, pineapple and cherries.

CRANBERRY SALAD

1 bag cranberries, frozen
1 bag miniature marshmallows
2 small bags or 1 large bag pecan pieces
2 cartons cool whip
6 medium, hard, red apples, chopped fine
Grind cranberries while frozen

Mix together with ½ cup sugar and refrigerate.

PINAPPLE DESSERT

In a large bowl, mix a 16 oz. can of crushed pineapple, un-drained, into a box of angel food cake mix.
Add 1 teaspoon vanilla

MaryAnn Sadler

Pour into a (LIGHTLEY) greased 9 by 13 pan and bake 350 for about 35 minutes or until golden brown.

CHERRY CAKE SQUARES

1 box white cake mix.
1 and ¼ cups rolled oats
½ cup softened margarine
1 egg
1 can cherry pie filling
½ cup chopped nuts (I like walnuts)
¼ cup packed brown sugar
Pre Heat oven to 350

Mix cake mix, 6 tablespoons margarine, 1 up oats.
Mix until it becomes crumbly.
Save 1 cup of the crumbly for toping.
To the remainder of the crumbly, add 1 egg and mix well.
Pour into a buttered or greased, or sprayed pan.
Pour the pie mix over this, spreading it so it covers all the mixture.

To the 1 cup of saved crumbly, add the remaining ¼ cup of oats
2 tablespoons marg., nuts and brown sugar
Spread on top of the cherry pie mix
Bake at 350 for 30 minutes or until golden
Cool and cut into squares.

GRHAM CRACKER PUDDING DELIGHT
(One of Jennifer's favorite's)

Line a nine inch square pan with graham crackers
Prepare a small pkg. of vanilla flavor instant pudding
and pie filling as directed on pkg.
Let it set until starts to thicken about 5 minutes.
Blend in 1 cup of cool whip to the pudding
Spread half of this over the graham crackers
Add another layer of graham crackers
Spread the rest of the pudding mixture over this layer.
Add another layer of graham crackers
Spread a can of cherry pie filling over the top layer of
graham crackers
Chill until ready to serve.

CAKES

CHEESE CAKE
(Deven's, Mine and Robert's Favorite)

1 graham cracker crust or make your own.
1 (8oz.) pack. Cream cheese, softened
1 (14oz.) Can sweetened condensed milk
⅓ cup lemon juice
1 teaspoon vanilla
Beat cheese until fluffily. Add milk. Mix thoroughly. Stir in lemon juice and vanilla. Pour into crust. Chill at least 2 hours.
You can pour a can of cherry pie filling on top, but don't invite Deven if you do.

MANDARIN ORANGE CAKE
(Sharity's favorites)

1 yellow cake mix
¾ cup oil
3 eggs

1 cup of Mandarin oranges and juice. Add enough of the juice to make the level 1 cup.

Add oil, eggs and oranges to cake mix. Beat until well blended. Bake in greased or sprayed 9 x 13 pan at 350 for 30 to 40 minutes. Watch it and let it get just golden brown.

TOPPING

Mix 1 (9oz.) carton of cool whip to 1 pak, (2 pie size), vanilla pudding with 1 small can of crushed pineapple (drained). Spread on top of the cool cake.

HUMMINGBIRD CAKE

2 cups sugar	1&½ cups butter flavored vegetable oil
3 eggs	3 cups flour
1 teaspoon baking soda	1 teaspoon salt
1 teaspoon cinnamon	1 small can crushed pineapple, do not drain
2 ripe bananas, mashed	1 cup chopped pecans

Mix all the dry ingredients together. Add the oil and the pineapple. Mix this up well.

Add the bananas and the nuts. Bake at 350 for just about one hour, or until golden brown, and finger touch to top of cake. Toothpick test doesn't do too well. Let cool, serve with whipped cream or cool whip.

PINEAPPLE UPSIDE DOWN CAKE

¼ cup softened margarine
¼ cup sugar   ¼ cup light brown sugar
½ cup dark Karo syrup   12 slices pineapple
1 pkg. white cake mix

Preheat oven to temperature directed on cake mix pkg. Blend margarine, sugar, syrup in a 13 X 9 X 2in. pan. Arrange pineapple on mixture. Heat in oven 15min. Meanwhile mix cake batter as directed on pack.
Remove pan from oven, pour batter carefully over fruit. Bake 45 to 55 min. or until cake is done. Remove from oven. Invert. Let stand one min. Remove pan.

EASTER BASKETS

Bake cup cakes. Decorate with colored coconut, jelly beans. Use pipe cleaners as handles.

STIR UP CHOCOLATE CAKE

1 ½ cups flour   1 beaten egg
1 teaspoon baking soda   ¾ cup veg. oil
1 cup sugar   1 teaspoon vanilla

¼ teaspoon salt   1 cup buttermilk
⅓ cup cocoa

Mix dry ingredients in a bowl. Add oil and stir. Add milk and mix thoroughly. Add beaten egg and vanilla. Bake at 350 for 20 minutes.

APPLE NUT CAKE

1 ⅓ cup oil   2 CUPS SUGAR

2 eggs   ¼ cup ground raisins

3 cups flour   1 teaspoon salt

1 teaspoon baking soda   3 cups peeled chopped
                                apples

1 teaspoon vanilla   2 teaspoons cinnamon
                                1cup chopped nuts

Mix oil, sugar, eggs together. Add flour, salt, soda, cinnamon, apples, raisins, nuts and vanilla. Bake I hour at 350. In a well-greased pan

OLD FASHIONED DEVIL'S FOOD.

Makes two 8″ layers

In a large bowl, mix
1 ¾ cups cake flour   1 ½ cups sugar

1 teaspoon salt   ½ cup cocoa

                        4 teaspoons baking powder

Add ⅔ cup vegetable shortening and ⅔ cup milk
Beat 2 minutes at medium speed with electric mixer.
Add ⅓ cup milk
2 eggs unbeaten
1 teaspoon vanilla
Beat 2 min. longer
Bake at 350degrees about 30 minutes in a well-greased
pan.

OATMEAL CAKE

1 ⅓ cup hot water pour over 1 cup oats.
Let stand 20 min.   2 eggs
½ cup shortening   1 cup brown sugar
1 cup white sugar   ½ teaspoon cinnamon
1 teaspoon baking soda   1 ⅓ cups flour
½ teaspoon salt

TOPPING

¾ stick margarine   1 teaspoon vanilla
1 cup brown sugar   1 cup nuts
¼ cup milk or cream   1 cup coconut
Heat topping ingredients until butter melts. Spread on
cake and return to oven for 5 min.

BANANA SPLIT CAKE

1 stick melted margarine	2 cups crushed graham cracker
4 bananas	2 sticks margarine
1reg. can crushed pineapple	2 eggs
Carton Cool Whip	½ cup chopped pecans
2cups powdered sugar	½ cup chopped Maraschino cherries

Mix melted margarine and graham crackers together and pat into a 13 x 9 x 2 inch pan. Beat the 2 sticks margarine, eggs and powered sugar with electric mixer for 15 min. Spread over unbaked crust. Cover with 4 bananas, sliced lengthwise and the drained pineapple. Cover with cool whip. Sprinkle with pecans and cherries. Reg. overnite.

BANANA CAKE

Make a crust of 1 stick of butter and 2 cups of graham cracker crust. Press this into a 13x9 cake pan.
Beat together 2 sticks of butter, 2 eggs, and 2 cups of powdered sugar until real smooth. Usually takes about 10 minutes beating time. Spread this over the graham cracker crust.

Slice 3 or 4 bananas over this. Pour a large can crushed, drained pineapple over the bananas. Cover this with whipped cream or cool whip. Sprinkle this with crushed pecans or walnuts. Keep in refrigerator until ready to serve.

You can also make a smaller one using a store bought graham cracker pie crust, and
by reducing the ingredients.

CHOPE SUEY CAKE

2 cups flour	2 cups sugar
2 teaspoon baking soda	½ teaspoon salt
2 eggs, beaten	1 cup chopped nuts
1 (20 oz.) can crushed pineapple, and juice	

Mix all ingredients well. Bake in greased and floured pan 9X13 for 35 to 40 minutes.

Frosting: 1 (8oz.) pk. Cream cheese 1 stick marg.
2 cups powdered sugar 1 teaspoon vanilla

FROSTINGS

CHOCOLATE CREAM CHEESE FROSTING

1 - 8oz. Pkg. cream cheese, softened
½ cup margarine, softened

2 teaspoons vanilla
6 and ½ cups powdered sugar
⅓ cup unsweetened cocoa powder
1 to 2 tablespoons milk or cream
Beat together cream cheese, butter, and vanilla until fluffy. Gradually add 2 cups powdered sugar and cocoa beating well. Gradually beat in rest of sugar until smooth. Beat in milk or cream if needed to make it spreadable.

PEANUT BUTTER FROSTING
Especially good on Spice Cake

¼ cup margarine   2 ½ cups powdered sugar
⅓ cup peanut butter   ½ cup cold coffee
⅛ teaspoon salt   ¼ teaspoon vanilla

Stir or beat margarine, peanut butter and salt until smooth.
Add sugar and coffee, alternately, a little at a time.
Mix thoroughly after each addition.
Stir in vanilla.

MARSHMALLOW FROSTING

½ cup sugar   small jar marshmallow crème
2 egg whites
2 Tablespoon water   ½ teaspoon vanilla

Combine sugar, egg whites and water in a double boiler.

Beat with electric mixer over boiling water until soft peaks form.

Add marshmallow crème, continue beating until stiff peaks form.

PIES

FRESH BLUEBERRY PIE
(Grandpa Ken really enjoyed this one)

4 cups blueberries
¾ cups water
1 tablespoon butter or margarine
¾ cup sugar
3 tablespoons cornstarch or 2 of flour
Dash of salt
1 teaspoon lemon juice
1 baked pie shell

In pan, combine 1 cup blueberries, water and butter. Bring to a simmer and simmer for 4 minutes. Combine the sugar, cornstarch or flour and salt, and add to the mixture in the pan. Bring to a boil over medium heat, stirring constantly. Cook and stir for 2 minutes. Stir in lemon juice and remaining blueberries. Pour into the baked pie shell. Chill for at least 2 or 3 hours. Serve with ice cream or cool whip.

RAISIN PIE
(This is the favorite one of Grandpa Ken's)

1 cup raisins
1 cup water
1 cup sugar
¼ cup butter or margarine
3 tablespoons flour
½ can of condensed milk

Combine raisins, water and sugar. Boil for 5 minutes. Mix condensed milk and flour to make a paste. Slowly stir the paste into the raisin mixture. Add the butter. Cook slowly stirring constantly until it thickens. Pour into a pie shell. Top with another pie shell. Bake at 350 until the crust is lightly brown.

LEMON CHEESCAKE PIE
(One of mine and Robert's favorites)

Beat 8 oz. softened cream cheese until smooth
Add 2 cups of cold milk, slowly
Beat until blended
Add instant lemon pudding mix, 1 pie size
Beat approx. 1 minute
Pour into a 9 in. graham cracker curst
Top with graham cracker crumbs if desired, or top with a can of cherry pie mix.

PEANUT BUTTER PIE

1 pk. 8oz. Cream cheese
1 cup peanut butter
1 cup sugar
1 tablespoon marg. softened
1 teaspoon vanilla
1 small carton Cool Whip.

Beat everything together except the cool whip, until smooth
Stir in the cool whip.
Spoon all this into a graham cracker crust
Choose your own topping if you want one.

RHUBARB PIE
(One of mine and Robert's favorites)

Mix 1 ⅛ cup sugar with 2 tablespoons flour, and a pinch of salt.
Mix this with 3 cups of rhubarb that you have cut up into about 1 inch pieces.
Put all this into a pie shell.
Dot with 2 tablespoons butter
Put a top crust on and make slashes in the top.
Bake at 425 for about 40 minutes.

CRANBERRY PIE
(One of Grandma Burton's favorites)

1 (8 oz.) pkg. Cream cheese softened
1 cup or 1 small carton of Cool Whip
¼ cup sugar
½ teaspoon vanilla
1 can whole berry cranberry sauce
1 graham cracker crust

Beat cream cheese until fluffy.

In separate bowl, beat cool whip, sugar and vanilla until peaks form
Beat the cream cheese mixture into the cool whip mixture until smooth
Save 2 tablespoons cranberry sauce, fold the remaining sauce into the whipped mixture.
Spoon into the pie crust and garnish the top with the 2 tablespoons of cranberry sauce you saved. Freeze about 2 hours.

GERMAN CHOCOLATE PIE

1 cup sugar
2 Tablespoons flour
2 tablespoons cocoa
Pinch of salt
2 eggs

3 tablespoons margarine, melted
⅔ cup milk
¾ cup shredded coconut
½ cup pecans, chopped
1 teaspoon vanilla

Combine all the dry ingredients. Stir in eggs, melted margarine and milk. Add coconut, vanilla and pecans. Mix well, pour into unbaked pie shell. Bake 30 minutes at 400 degrees.

CANDY PIE

In the microwave, cook about 1 min., ¼ cup butter and 4 cups small marshmallows. Stir until marshmallows are melted. You may have to reheat a minute. Add 6 cups rice Krispy cereal. Mix well, press this onto the bottom and sides of 2 greased 9 in. pie plates. Melt 1 and ⅓ cups chocolate pieces. Pour into the pressed mixture. Sprinkle with 2 cups peanut butter pieces. Chill until set.

STRAWBERRY PIE
(Robert's favorite)

¾ cup water
1 cup sugar
¼ teaspoon salt

1 teaspoon lemon juice

3 tablespoon cornstarch (you can use 6 tablespoons flour, but cornstarch is best)

1 (3oz) package strawberry Jell-O

1 qt. strawberries sliced

Mix cornstarch, sugar and salt together.

Stir in the water, boil until it get turns clear, if using cornstarch or until it gets thick if using flour.

Remove from heat and stir in the package of Jell-O. Cool completely.

Place sliced strawberries in a 9-inch baked pie crust, using enough strawberries to fill the pie crust.

Pour the cooked mixture over the strawberries. Chill until set. Top with cool whip, if desired.

CREAM CHEESE BROWNIE PIE

I refrigerated pie crust, softened

1 8oz. Pkg. cream cheese, softened

3 tablespoons sugar

3 eggs

1 pkg. thick and fuggy hot fudge swirl deluxe brownie mix

¼/cup oil

2 tablespoons water

½ cup chopped pecans

Heat oven to 350 degrees

In medium bowl, combine cream cheese, sugar, vanilla and 1 egg

Beat until smooth. Set aside.

Reserve the hot fudge pk. from the brownie mix for topping.

In a large bowl, combine the brownie mix, oil, 1 tablespoon water and 2 eggs.

Beat well with a spoon.

Spread ½ cup of the brownie mixture in the pie crust. (Of course the crust must be in a pie plate.) Thought I forgot that didn't you?

Spoon and carefully spread cream cheese mixture over the brownie mixture that is in the pie crust.

Top with the other half of the brownie mixture. Spread this evenly.

Sprinkle on the pecans.

Bake at 350degrees for about 45 minutes, or until the center is golden brown

Place the hot fudge from the packet in a bowl, microwave for about 30 seconds.

Stir in 1tablespoon water. Slowly pour this over the top of the pie. Cool completely

CANDY

MARSHMALLOW FUDGE

3 cups sugar

1 cup cream

2 (6oz.) pack. Chocolate chips or 2 cups

1 teaspoon vanilla

⅓ cup butter or margarine

1 jar marshmallow crème 6 or 8 oz

1 cup nuts, if you wish

Combine sugar, butter, cream and marshmallow crème in a heavy saucepan, that want allow burn so easy. Heat slowly to boil, stirring frequently. Don't forget to stir.

When mixture boils, so that you can't stop the boil by stirring, time 4 minutes, stirring constantly

Remove from heat, stir in chocolate chips, just until melted.

Add the nuts and vanilla.

Pour this into a buttered or sprayed pan. COOL.

Cut into squares. I find a pizza cutter does best.

If you like something different, you can use butterscotch chips or peanut butter chips instead of the chocolate chips.

PEANUT BRITTLE

(Kenny's favorite, also was grandpa Ken's favorite.)

2 cups sugar

1 cup light corn syrup

½ cup water

¼ cup dark molasses

2 tablespoons butter

2 cups salted peanuts

1 tablespoon baking soda

Combine sugar, syrup and water in a 3 quart saucepan. While bringing to a boil, stir <u>just</u> until sugar has melted and it turns clear. Using a candy thermometer, cook until temperature reaches 290 degrees

Remove from heat and quickly stir in molasses and butter.

Return to heat and continue cooking <u>without</u> stirring until the temperatures returns to 290 degrees.

Remove from heat. <u>Careful,</u> it is hot.

Quickly stir in peanuts and baking soda.

Quickly mix it up thoroughly.

Pour immediately onto a large buttered or sprayed metal cookie sheet. Allow it to cool completely.

Break into small pieces.

Notice I put quickly in different places, that's because you have to move fast before the candy gets hard. Be careful, because you can get burnt.

PEANUT BUTTER OR
CHOCOLATE FUDGE

3 cups sugar	⅓ cup butter or margarine
1 cup cream	1 jar marshmallow crème (6 OR 8 oz. size)

2 (6 OZ.) pk. Chocolate chips or peanut butter chips, OR 2 cups

1 cup chopped nuts	1 teaspoon vanilla

Combine sugar, butter, cream, marshmallow crème in a heavy saucepan. Heat slowly to boil, stirring frequently.

When mixture boils so that boiling cannot be stopped, by stirring, time for 4 minutes, stirring constantly

Remove from heat and stir in the chips until melted.

Add the nuts and vanilla.

Pour into a buttered or sprayed 11x11 pan. Cool completely before cutting.

I like to use a pizza cutter to cut it with.

MARSHMALLOW CRÈME FUDGE

3 cups sugar
1 cup evaporated milk or can of cream
1 pint jar of marshmallow crème
¾ stick butter or marg.
1(12oz.) pack of chocolate chips
1 cup chopped walnuts

Bring sugar, milk and butter to a boil. Cook to 236 on candy thermometer, stirring often. Remove from heat. Instantly stir in marshmallow crème, nuts and chocolate chips. Stir until marshmallow crème and chocolate chips are melted. Pour into a buttered pan. Let cool and cut into squares.

PEANUT BUTTER CUPS
(Deven truly fell in love with this one)

Melt chocolate candy bars, or chocolate chips in a pan on top of the stove, on low heat, stirring often.
Place miniature cupcake holders in a muffin pan.
Pour miniature cupcake holders half full of melted chocolate.
Put a teaspoon of peanut butter on top of chocolate.
Finish with melted chocolate on top of peanut butter.
Chill or freeze until firm.

DIVINITY

3 cups sugar

1 cup light corn syrup

2 stiff beaten egg whites

1 cup water

½ cup chopped walnuts

1 teaspoon vanilla

dash of salt

Boil together the sugar, corn syrup and water to medium ball stage (246) stirring only until sugar is dissolved. Watch the candy thermometer, as the temp. raises fast. When the thermometer shows 246, remove the pan from heat and slowly pour over stiff beaten egg whites, beating constantly.

Continue to beat until mixture is no longer hot, about 10 minutes. Add remaining ingredients. Allow to cool until mixture holds its shape when dropped from a spoon. Drop from a spoon onto waxed paper.

COCOA FUDGE

2 cups cocoa

¼ cup butter

1 ½ cups milk

⅛ teaspoon salt

3 cups sugar

1 teaspoon vanilla

Combine cocoa, sugar and salt in a large (3qt) size pan. Add milk gradually, mix thoroughly, bring to a bubbly boil on high heat, stirring constantly. Reduce heat to medium and continue to boil the mixture without stirring, until it reaches a temperature of 234 or until a small amount of mixture forms a stiff ball when dropped into cold water.

Be sure the thermometer is not touching the bottom of the pan or u will get a bad reading. Remove the pan from heat, add butter and vanilla to mixture DO NOT STIR. Set saucepan in cold water to hasten cooling. Cool to 110. Beat by hand or with portable mixer until the fudge thickens and loses some of the shine. Quickly pour and spread fudge in a lightly buttered pan. Cool. Cut into squares,

BUTTER-NUT CRUNCH

1 cup butter, anytime my recipes calls for butter, u can use margarine.

1 cup sugar   2 tablespoon water
1 tablespoon light corn syrup   ¾ cup chopped nuts

Melt butter. Remove from heat.
Add sugar and stir well. Put in the thermometer.
Stir mixture well and after the bubbling starts add water and syrup. Then stir often. Cook until mixture reaches 290. Gradually stir in nuts and pour into a buttered pan. Melt chocolate chips. Spread over the mixture in the pan. When cooled, break into pieces.

SODA CRACKER FUDGE

2 cups sugar   27 crushed soda crackers
⅔ cups milk   1 teaspoon vanilla
6 tablespoon peanut butter

Boil sugar and milk for 4 minutes on medium heat stirring so milk want burn. Remove from heat and add peanut butter. Stir until blended. Add crushed soda crackers, vanilla. Stir until thick. Drop on wax paper by a spoon full.

COOKIES

COCONUT MACAROONS
(Grandpa Ken's Favorite)

1 cup Eagle Brand Milk
4 Cups shredded coconut
1 teaspoon vanilla
4 ¾ teaspoon almond extract
Mix all the ingredients together
Drop teaspoon full of this mixture about an inch apart
on a sprayed or greased baking sheet.
Bake 350 degrees about 8 minutes or until they are
lightly brown. Don't over bake.

BASIC COOKIE DOUGH

½ cup soft butter or margarine
1 cup sugar
2 eggs
2 tablespoons cream
1 teaspoon vanilla

2 ½ cups flour
½ teaspoon salt
¼ teaspoon soda
Mix together margarine, sugar, eggs. Stir in cream and vanilla. Mix together dry ingredients and stir into the margarine mixture. Chill dough 4 or 5 hours
Heat oven to 375
Roll out dough a little at a time, keeping the rest chilled. Cut out cookies desired shapes. Bake about 6 minutes until lightly browned. Decorate anyway you want to.

CHERRY DREAM SQUARES

1 box white cake mix
1 ¼ cups oats
½ cup margarine, softened
1 egg

1 can cherry pie filling
½ cup chopped nuts
¼ cup packed brown sugar

Heat oven to 350, grease 13x9 pan
Mix cake mix, 6 tablespoons margarine, 1 cup oats, mix until crumbly. Save 1 cup crumbs for topping. To the remaining crumbs, add 1 egg. Mix well. Press into prepared pan. Top with cherry pie mix.
To reserved crumbs add remaining ¼ cup oats, 2 tablespoons margarine, nuts and brown sugar.

Mix well, sprinkle over cherry pie mixture. Bake for 30 min or until golden brown.

SUGAR COOKIES

Cream until light and fluffy ½ cup butter
Beat in ¾ cup sugar
Add I egg
2 teaspoons vanilla
Beat thoroughly.
Add 1¼ cup flour
¼ teaspoon salt
¼ teaspoon baking powder
Stir and blend well Arrange by a teaspoonful on buttered cookie sheet
Flatten slightly
Bake 8 min.

MARSHMALLOW TREATS

¼ cup butter
2 cups (I pint) marshmallow crème, OR 40 large marshmallows, OR 4 cups miniature marshmallows.
6 cups Rice Krispy's

Melt butter; add marshmallow crème or marshmallows, stirring constantly until blended. Stir in Rice Krispy's
Spread on a lightly buttered cookie sheet.

M AND M COOKIES

Beat thoroughly with a fork

1 cup shortening	Stir in
1 cup brown sugar packed.	2 ¼ cups all-purpose flour
½ cup granulated sugar	1 teaspoon baking soda
2 teaspoons vanilla	1 teaspoon salt
2 eggs	

Stir in about ½ cup M and M's plain chocolate candies.

Drop by a teaspoon full onto greased cookie sheet.

Decorate tops with M and M's.

Bake at 350 for 10 to 12 minutes or until golden brown

BOILED CHOCOLATE OATMEAL COOKIES

2 cups sugar	½ cup milk
¼ lb. margarine	2 tablespoon cocoa

Combine in a saucepan, bring to a hard boil, boil 2 minutes.

Remove from heat. Add 1 cup nuts, 2 cups of quick cooking oats, 1 teaspoon vanilla. Spoon out on was paper and let cool.

FINGERS

2 sticks of margarine   2 cup pecans chopped pecans
½ cup sugar   2 ½ cups flour
1 tablespoon vanilla   powdered sugar

Have margarine room temp. Mix margarine, sugar, vanilla and flour. It will be heavy. Add pecans and roll out in small finger like rolls.
Bake on ungreased cookie sheet I hour at 250. Remove from oven and roll immediately in powdered sugar.
After cooled, roll again in powdered sugar.

PINEAPPLE COOKIES

Mix thoroughly
1 cup soft shortening
⅔ cup sugar
1 egg
Stir in
1 (9oz.) 1 cup, can crushed pineapple with the juice

Mix together
3 ½ cups flour
1 teaspoon baking soda
½ teaspoon salt
¼ teaspoon nutmeg
Stir the dry ingredients into the egg mixture
Stir in ½ cup chopped nuts

MaryAnn Sadler

Chill at least one hour
Drop by a rounded teaspoon full about 1 in. apart on a
lightly greased baking sheet
Bake at 400 for 8 to 10min.s or until when touched
lightly with finger no imprint remains

PEANUT BUTTER COOKIES

3 cups flour
2 teaspoons baking soda
¼ teaspoon salt
1 cup shortening
1 cup sugar

1 cup brown sugar, packed
2 eggs beaten
1 cup peanut butter
1 teaspoon vanilla

Mix ingredients as listed to a stiff batter. Form into balls,
press onto greased cookie sheet. Press with the back of
a fork to make a cress cross designs Bake 10 minutes at
375 degrees. Remove from sheet immediately.

BUTTERDCOTCH COOKIE BARS

½ cup margarine

1 ½ cups graham cracker
crumbs

1 (14 oz.) can Eagle Brand Sweetened Condensed
Milk 1 cup (6 oz.) sweet chocolate chips

1 cup (6oz.) Butterscotch
chips

1 cup coconut

Preheat oven to 350

In 13 x9 inch pan, melt margarine in oven.

Sprinkle graham Cracker crumbs over melted margarine

Pour Eagle Brand evenly over the crumbs.

Top with remaining ingredients. Press down. Bake 25 to 30 minutes or until lightly browned.

Cool. Cut into squares

PECAN TASSIES

1 (3oz.) pk cream cheese	½ cup margarine
1 cup flour	1 egg
¾ cup packed brown sugar	1 teaspoon vanilla
¾ cup (chopped real fine) pecans	

Blend softened cream cheese and margarine.

Stir in flour

Chill

Divide dough into 24 balls

Press onto bottom and sides of miniature muffin pans.

Combine egg, brown sugar and vanilla

Stir in the nuts

Fill cups ¾ full of the mixture

Bake at 325 for 25 to 30 minutes or until lightly brown

Cool 5 min. Remove from pans.

CANNING

CANNED APPLE PIE FILLING
(Mariann's favorite)

6 cups sugar

2 ¼ teaspoons cinnamon

1 teaspoon salt

3 tablespoons lemon juice

2 cups flour

2 ¼ teaspoon nutmeg

10 cups water

3 Tablespoons butter

Peel and slice enough apples to fill 7 quart jars. Put the sliced apples in the jars. After the jars are all full, place a canner at least ⅔ full of water on to heat. In a large pan, mix sugar, flour, cinnamon, and nutmeg and salt thoroughly. Slowly stir in the 10 cups of water. Cook until this starts to thicken.

Remove from the heat and stir in the lemon juice and butter.

Pour this over the apples in the jars.

Wipe the tops of the jars off real good, with a wet cloth. Seal

Place the hot jars in water that you should have already heating on the stove.

If the water isn't as hot as the jars of apples, your jars will burst.

As soon as the water starts to boil, reduce heat and simmer for 20 minutes.

Carefully remove the jars from the hot water.

Place on a counter away from any draft and allow to cool at least 24 hours before you store them.

FIG APPLE JAM
(Makes a great glaze for ham)

Wash and scald 6 (8oz.) Jars

1 lb. pack dried fig pieces
2 sour apples
The peeling of 1 orange
The peeling of 1 lemon
Squeeze the juice from the lemon and the orange, save.
3 cups sugar
4 cups water
Dash of salt

Remove the white parts inside the peelings of the orange and the lemon. Put figs, apples, orange and lemon peelings through a grinder. Place the mixture in a heavy saucepan. Add the water and boil for 10 minutes. Reduce the heat to simmer and cook and additional 10 minutes. Add the sugar and salt. Mix well and simmer an additional 20 minutes, stirring often. Don't forget to stir, often. Add the juice from the lemon and the orange and mix this well. Pour into the hot scalded jars. Wipe top of jars with damp cloth, seal. Let cool 24 hours before storing.

HOT PEEPER JELLY

1 jalapeno pepper seeded and chopped fine. (Please wear gloves to seed and chop this pepper)
7 medium green bell peppers cut in about 1 inch pieces with the white part and the seeds removed.
1 and ½ cups cider vinegar
¼ teaspoon canning salt
1 package Pectin
5 cups sugar
1 and ½ cups apple juice
About 8 drops of green food coloring

Puree the jalapeno and the green peppers together. Add the vinegar and the apple juice. Mix well, cover and chill overnight, in a bowl. Do not use a metal pan, to soak overnight. Cover the bowl with a plate or aluminum foil. In the morning, put on a canner of water to heat as you will have to process the jars of jelly.

The water needs to be boiling when you place the jars into it. In a colander, strain the mixture that has been soaking all night. Measure 4 cups of the juice, you drained off, in a large kettle.

Add enough water to make the 4 cups, if need be. Stir in the Pectin and salt. Bring to a rolling boil. Boil 1 minute stirring constantly.

Remove from heat, stir in food coloring. Pour into hot jars. Wipe tops with damp cloth and seal.

Place the hot jars in the hot canner of boiling water, **please be careful**. Turn off heat under canner, place lid on canner and let sit for 5 minutes.

Remove the jars from the canner and let rest on counter on a dish cloth for at least 24 hours before checking to make sure all jars are sealed. You can now store your jelly.

APPLE PIE JELLY

5 cups apple juice
1 teaspoon cinnamon
1 teaspoon nutmeg
½ teaspoon cloves
1 pkg. Sure-Jel
Follow directions on Sure-Jel pkg. for apple juice.
You may need to add juice or re-duce to use pectin.
Use amount of sugar the pkg. calls for.

SAUERKRAUT

1 teaspoon salt
1 teaspoon sugar
1 teaspoon vinegar
Cut up cabbage and pack in quart jars.
Add the salt, sugar and vinegar. Pour boiling water in the jars of cabbage. Leave about an inch of space at the top of the jar as the kraut needs to expand. Seal and store in a cool dark place. It should be ready to use in about 3 weeks. It will run off. This is Grandma Burton's recipe.

GREEN TOMATOE PICKLES
(Grandma Iva Sadler's recipe

2 quart small green tomatoes or cut larger ones in 4 pieces
2 cups chopped onions
¾ cup hot pepper, chopped
2 cups sugar
3 tablespoons salt
Remember to always use canning salt when canning. Regular salt will let you can goods spoil.)
2 cups white vinegar
1 teaspoon celery seed

Put tomatoes, onions and hot peppers in a large pan. Mix remaining ingredients together. And pour over the tomatoes. Cook only to a boil. Remove from heat immediately. Put in hot jars, seal. Allow to cool 24 hours and check for seal before storing. This is Grandma Iva Sadler's recipe.

They can also be canned, using **My Dill Pickle Recipe**.

ASPARAGUS

Remove scales from the stalks. Wash. Cut in the length of the jar you are using. Tie the asparagus in bundles. Place the tips in boiling water, just enough to cover the tough parts. Cover and boil 3 minutes. Drain and pack in hot jars. Add ½ teaspoon canning salt to each pint jar. Fill to within ½ inch of top of jar, with water that you cooked the asparagus in. Wipe top of jars with clean, damp cloth. Seal and put in canner of boiling water and cook on low heat for 30 minutes. Place on counter for 24 hours before storing. (Anytime you place hot jars on your counter, place them on a dry dish cloth to protect your counter.)

MY DILL PICKLES

1 cup white vinegar
3 cups water
¼ cup canning salt
1 teaspoon alum

Pack small cucumbers in jars. Place a sprig of dill **or** a teaspoon of dill seed, a clove of garlic, small stalk of celery, 1 small hot pepper **or** ½ teaspoon of crushed red pepper in each jar. Heat the vinegar, water, salt and alum to boil. Pour over cucumbers, wipe top of jar with clean damp cloth and seal.

A canner of water should be on to boil as you pack the cucumbers. Place the jars of cucumbers in the boiling water, turn off heat, and let them set in the water for 5 minutes for pints and 10 minutes if you use quarts.
Remove from canner and place on counter for 24 hours before disturbing them.
Check for seal and store. If jars didn't sealed, store in frig. for about a week, before using.

OKRA

Use same recipe as MY DILL PICKLES

CELERY

Use same recipe as MY DILL PICKLES

PICKLED GREEN TOMATOES

Use same recipe as MY DILL PICKLES

CANNED GREEN BEANS

Wash the beans good
Break the beans into about 1 inch pieces
Put in colander and rinse again.
Pack the beans in jars, about ½ inch from top of jar.
To each pint jar, place ½ teaspoon canning salt. Quarts place 1 teaspoon salt.
Salt may be left out if you wish. Fill the jar with water. Run a knife down inside the jar to get rid of air bubbles. Wipe the top of the jar with a damp cloth, place on lid, and tighten hand tight.
Put jars in canner, of water, cover with lid, bring to a boil, reduce temp.
Simmer and time for 3 hours. You can simmer them for only two and one half hours and then let them let set in the hot water for a couple hours. This will save gas.
Remove from cooker to counter and let set for 24 hours, before storing.

You can also make dill green beans using MY RECIPE FOR DILL PICKLES

HOT PEPPER PIECES
(Mine, Bob's Sharity's and Jim's favorite)

<u>You Must Wear Gloves</u>

Cut hot peppers in to pieces and soak them over night in ¼ cup of canning salt to 1 gallon of water. Use a bowl to soak them over night in, don't use a metal pan. Cover the bowl with a plate or aluminum foil. Next morning, put a **canner** of water on to heat to process the peppers in. Drain the peppers in a colander, pack them in jars. (Please wear gloves while handling hot peppers at all times.) In a separate pan put

> ¼ cup canning salt
>
> 1 cup white vinegar
>
> 3 cups water
>
> 1 teaspoon alum

Bring the salt, vinegar, alum and water to a boil. Pour this over the peppers in the jars, Seal. Place the hot jars in the hot canner of water, (Water in **canner** must be boiling when you put the jars of peppers in it). Cover with lid.

Turn off the heat, let set for 5 minutes. (If you don't turn off the heat the peppers will be soft.) Remove from canner

Let sit on counter for at least 24 hours before storing.

APPLE BUTTER
(My Sister, Daisy's, favorite)

About eight peeled apples

2 and ½ cups sugar (or 2 cups sugar and ½ cup brown sugar)

2 and ½ teaspoon cinnamon

½ teaspoon cloves

¼ teaspoon salt

½ teaspoon allspice

Simmer about 12 hours in crock pot. Pour into hot jars and seal. Let set 24 hours before storing. Make sure each jar is sealed before storing.

A quick trick to this. If you have canned apple sauce on hand, us it instead the apples and just put it on to cook with all the spices listed above and heat slowly to boiling and cook about 10 minutes on low heat stirring occasionally to prevent scorching, pour in hot jars and seal. Let set 24 hours before disturbing it and make sure jars are sealed after 24 hours before storing it away.

RASPBERRY APPLE BUTTER

20 apples, peeled and cut into small pieces

1 cup water

3 cups raspberries

4 cups sugar

1 teaspoon cinnamon

¼ teaspoon cloves

Mix this all together, put in a crock pot. Cook approx. 12 hours, stirring once in a while. Pack it hot, into hot jars. Seal and set for 24 hours. Check seal and store.

GOLDEN CORN RELISH
(Grandpa Ken's favorite relish)

2 quarts corn cut from cob.

1 quart chopped cabbage

1 and ¼ cups chopped onion

1 cup chopped green bell pepper

1 cup chopped red bell pepper

1 cup chopped celery

4 cups apple cider vinegar

1 and ½ cups sugar

1 cup water

2 tablespoons mustard seed

1 tablespoon salt

1 tablespoon ground turmeric

1 teaspoon celery seed

In a large pan, combine all ingredients.

Bring to a simmer and simmer about 20 minutes. Stir occasionally.

Pour vegetable mixture into hot jars. Put on lids.

While it is simmering, put a canner of water on to heat, bringing it to a boil. Place jars in the canner of boiling water, turn heat to low and let cook for 15 minutes. Remove from canner and set on counter for 24 hours before disturbing. After 24 hours, check for seal and store.

SQUASH RELISH

10 cups diced yellow or zucchini squash
4 cups onions, diced
1 cup bell peppers, red or green, diced.
5 tablespoons canning salt
Mix this altogether in a bowl and let it stand all night. Remember to never let any thing like this stand all night in a pan. Be sure to use a bowl. Cover it with a plate. In the morning, drain all the liquid off that you possibly can. Now, mix 2 and ½ cups of cider vinegar, 3 cups of sugar and 1 tablespoon celery seed together. Mix this to the squash that you just drained. Put all this in a large pan, bring to a boil, reduce the heat and just simmer slowly for 30 minutes. Pack in hot jars and seal. Remember, let all canned items sit for at least 24 hours and make sure the jars are sealed, before storing. If the center of the sealer is down, they are sealed.

TOMATOES

(Tomatoes and tomato juice is Kenny, Jr's favorite)

Wash tomatoes
Pour boiling water over them and let sit 3 minutes
Drain off water, carefully
Let cool slightly, skin the peeling off.
Cut in quarters or place whole in the jars.

Add ½ teaspoon of canning salt to quarts, ¼ teaspoon to pints.

Fill jars with water, running a butter knife down inside to make sure all air spaces are full with water.

Place jars in canner, cover with water, bring to boil, lower heat to simmer and let simmer for 30 minutes.

TOMATOE JUICE

Wash the tomatoes, cut out bad places, and scold them for 3 minutes in boiling water

Drain off the water, careful watching the steam as it will burn you.

Cut out stem and the peelings should just slide off.

Put tomatoes in a cooker and cook until they are like mush.

Press them through a colander,

After you got them made into juice, put the juice in jars, add ½ teaspoon canning salt to quart and ¼ to a pint, seal

Never forget to wipe top of jars with a damp cloth before sealing on anything you can.

Place in cooker and cover jars with water, bring to a boil, reduce heat to simmer and time 45 minutes.

PINEAPPLE ORANGE MARMALADE

Combine

3 oranges   2 lemons
2 ½ cups water   ⅛ teaspoon baking soda

Place 3 oranges, most of white removed, and 2 lemons white removed, in a processer until and peelings are pretty well grind to small pieces. Measure 5 cups of the pulp add a box of pectin. Bring to a hard boil, stir in 5 cups of sugar,
¼ teaspoon nutmeg
1 teaspoon butter
Return to hard boil and boil 1 min, stirring constantly.
Ladle in jars and process 10 min.

BEETS

This will make (24pints) from ½ bushel of beets
Boil beets 30-35 minutes, remove skins

Mix 8 cups apple cider vinegar
3 teaspoons pickling salt
4 cups sugar
4 cups water
Heat to boil, pour over beets that are already in jar and process 30 minutes

BEETS
Prepare same as above
These are canned with syrup
Mix together

2 cups sugar	1 teaspoon cloves
2 cups water	1 teaspoon allspice
2 cups apple cider vinegar	1 tablespoon cinnamon

Pour over the beets and boil 10 minutes. Pack into hot jars and seal.

BEETS LIKE MOM BURTON CANNED

Prepare the beets as above.
Mix together

⅛ cup canning salt	1 cup sugar
1 quart water	1 quart vinegar

Bring to a boil. Pour over vinegar in jars and seal. Process 30 min.

SWEET PEPPER PIECES

Cook in pieces; soak overnight in ¼ cup canning salt, ½ gallon water. Next morning, drain. Pack in jars. Make sure your jars are always hot when canning.

Heat to boil

2 cups vinegar	1 tablespoon mixed pickle spices

3 cups sugar   2 cups water
Pour over peppers and seal

ROTEL

1 gallon tomatoes, scolded, peeled, ready for canning
2 large bell peppers seeded and chopped fine
I large onion diced
8 Jalapeno peppers seeded and chopped fine
¾ cup apple cider vinegar
¼ cup sugar
1 ½ Tablespoons canning salt

Mix all ingredients, bring to a boil, and simmer for 45 minutes.
Add 1 tablespoon lemon juice to each jar.
Fill jars with hot mixture.
Process for 45 minutes

PICCALILLI
Makes 6 pints

1 quart chopped cabbage

1 qt. chopped green tomatoes

2 sweet red bell peppers chopped

2 sweet green bell peppers chopped

2 large onions chopped

¼ cup canning salt

1 ½ cups apple cider vinegar 1 ½ cups water

2 cups firmly packed brown 1 teaspoon. Dry mustard
sugar

1 teaspoon Turmeric   1 teaspoon celery seed

Mix veg. with the salt and let stand covered overnight
Next morning, drain and press out as much liquid as
possible.
Boil the vinegar, water, sugar and spices 5 minutes.
Add the vegetables, bring to a boil, and pack into jars
and seal.
Remember, no matter what u are canning, have your
jars in the sink filled with scolding water. Empty them
as you use them. Have you sealers sitting in hot water
also.

SALSA

10 cups of chopped tomatoes, you may also used
canned tomatoes

8 limes   2 Jalapeno peppers

2 large green tomatoes,   1 large onion
chopped

2 head of garlic chopped   1 Tablespoon cumin powder

Enough canning salt to   small amount of brown
taste   sugar

About half cup of apple cider vinegar

Mix all together, boil 20 minutes on low heat.
Pack in jars
Process 30 minutes

WATERMELON RIND PRESERVES
Makes about 6 ½ pints

I sliced it last time and canned it, didn't care for it. But,
I decided to grind it. It works better,

1 ½ quarts ground watermelon rind	4 Tablespoon canning salt
3 ½ quarts water, divided	1 tablespoon ground ginger
4 cups sugar	¼ cup lemon juice
½ cup thinly chopped lemon	

Trim the watermelon rind to remove the entire pink
Grind or chop the rind very fine
Dissolve salt in 2 quarts of water.
Pour the salted water over the rind. Let stand for 5 to
6 hours.
Drain, rinse, and drain again.
Cover rind with cold water and let sit 30 minutes.
Drain.

Sprinkle ginger over the rind. Cover with water. Cook about 20 minutes. Drain.

Combine sugar, lemon juice and 1 ½ quarts water in a large sauce pan. Add the rind and boil gently 30 minutes or until syrup thickens. Add lemon and cook until melon is transparent. Remove from heat. Ladle in hot jars. Seal and process 20 minutes.

SWEET PEPPER RELISH

12 red peppers	12 green peppers
12 onions	2 cups white vinegar
2 cups sugar	2 tablespoons canning salt

Grind peppers and onion
Mix with salt, sugar, vinegar and bring to a boil. Simmer 5 min. Pack in hot jars and seal

MY OWN RELISH

Grind al together

1 quart cabbage	1 quart tomatoes, green and red
4 peppers red and green	2 large onions
I stalk of celery	3 cucumbers

Mix with ¼ cup canning salt and let stand over night. Drain and squeeze out as much liquid as possible.

Mix 1 ½ cups apple cider vinegar 1½ cup water
2 cups firmly pack brown sugar or I box 1 teaspoon
dry mustard
1 teaspoon turmeric 1 teaspoon alum
1 teaspoon celery seed
Boil for 5 minutes
Add the chopped vegetables, bring to a boil and pour
into jars and seal immediately.

CANNED TURNIPS

Peel, quarter, put in jars, add ½ teaspoon salt.
Cover with water.
Wipe rim, seal and place in canner and process for 45
min.

DIPS

2 (8 OZ) pks Fruit flavored cream cheese
2 (7oz.) jars marshmallow cream
1 cool whip
Cream the cream cheese, add marshmallow cream
Blend well
Add cool whip
Serve with chunks of fruit.

BLACK BEAN AND CORN SALSA (One of Robert and Sharity's favorite)

¼ cup mayonnaise
2 tablespoons lime juice
½ teaspoon ground cumin
1 can (19 oz.) black beans drain them in a colander and then rinse them
1 can (11 oz.) whole kernel corn, drained
1 cup, sliced in half, grape tomatoes
½ cup chopped red onion
2 tablespoon chopped, fresh, cilantro
1 teaspoon chopped jalapeno pepper

In a bowl, mix mayonnaise, lime juice and cumin, together.

Stir in the rest of the ingredients.

Use chips to dip it with.

GUACOMOLE DIP
(Sharity loves guacamole and so does me)

2 ripe avocados	⅓ teaspoon crushed red pepper
1 teaspoon salt	½ tablespoon grated onion
1 and ½ teaspoon lemon juice	1 teaspoon Worcestershire sauce
1 clove garlic, grated	

Peel and mash the avocados. Add salt and lemon juice. Stir in Worcestershire sauce, garlic, pepper and onion.

FRUIT DIP

2 (8oz.) pkgs. Fruit flavored cream cheese
2 (7oz.) jars marshmallow crème
1 small container cool whip

Cream the cream cheese, add the marshmallow crème, and blend well. Add the cool whip. Serve with chunks of cantaloupe, honey dew melon, pineapple, apple, strawberries or grapes. I especially liked the apples dipped in it.

CHESSE AND SALSA DIP

1 lb of cheese your choice
1 cup of Salsa, your choice
Heat 5 minutes or until cheese has melted and blended with the salsa, stirring constantly

MICELLANOUS

LYE SOAP

BE VERY CAREFUL MAKING THIS BREATHING THE LYE IS ALSO TOXIC

1 cup lye

2 qt. grease. Lard is best

1 cup ammonia

2 heaping tablespoons Borax

1 qt. water

Dissolve the lye in 1 qt. cold water. Warm the grease, and strain if using used grease. When both the lye and the grease are cool, stir the grease into lye and then add the Borax that has been dissolved in a little water, and the ammonia. Stir until it gets thick, about like honey. Pour into a tray lined with wax paper. Cut into squares before it gets too cold. A cardboard box is best used as a tray.

MaryAnn Sadler

NOTES

I hope you all really enjoy these recipes. I always loved to cook and I was always experimenting with recipes. If something doesn't suit your taste, don't be afraid to play with a recipe until it does. Add a smidgen of this or a dab of that until it suits your taste.

Sour nats nits a problem? Sit a cup of apple cider vinegar where they are and they will drown themselves.

Whip the cake frosting you buy in those little containers for a few minutes. It will almost double itself in size.

If ants or a bother, place a small amount of cornmeal in their path. They carry it back to the nest and it swells in them and they die.

Sprinkle your plants with cayenne pepper to keep squirrels away.

Carry a dryer sheet in your pocket to keep mosquitoes away.